ROBERT BURTON

ANIMAL HOMES

SEASHORE

photographs by Oxford Scientific Films

Newington Press

First published in the United States
in 1991 by Newington Press
2 Old New Milford Road
Brookfield, Connecticut 06804

First published in Great Britain in
1991 by Belitha Press Limited

Words in **bold** are explained in the
glossary at the end of this book.

Cataloging-in-Publication Data

Burton, Robert
Animal homes: Seashore / Robert Burton;
photographs by Oxford Scientific Films.
Brookfield, CT, Newington Press, 1991.

24 p.; ill.:
Includes glossary and index.
ISBN 1-878137-19-0

1. Marine animals. 2. Animal babies.
3. Animal defenses. 4. Animals—Food.
I. Title. II. Oxford Scientific Films,
photographers.
591.92
Bur

The seashore is the border between the sea and the land. As the tide goes in and out each day, the animals living on the seashore are sometimes underwater and sometimes on land. Some hide in **tide pools,** where the water is trapped after the tide has gone out.

Some animals, such as fish, visit the shore only when the tide is in because they cannot live out of the water. Fish usually live in deeper water, but sometimes they can be found in pools on the shore. Other animals spend their whole lives on the shore.

The common periwinkle (above) is a kind of snail that lives on rocks. It eats seaweed at **high tide.** When the tide goes out, the periwinkle stays inside its shell. Even though it is out of the water, its body does not dry up.

Shore crabs can be recognized by the notches on the front edges of their shells. The back pair of the crab's ten legs are flattened, like paddles. Crabs are **predators.** Shore crabs eat periwinkles and other small animals that they seize with their powerful, sharp **pincers.** They also feed on dead animals.

Shore crabs spend the day close to rocks or among seaweed, where they cannot easily be seen. They can defend themselves with their pincers. However, some crabs are eaten by bigger predators, such as birds and large fish. If a crab loses a leg or pincer to a predator, it can grow a new one to replace it.

Female crabs carry their eggs under their tails. After the baby crabs hatch, they float in the sea before settling on shore.

Limpets are a bit like snails and periwinkles. All these animals have a soft, flat foot that they use for crawling slowly over the ground. The main difference between a limpet and a snail is that a limpet's shell is shaped like a cone, and a snail's shell is coiled. When the tide is out, limpets hold tightly to the rocks. It takes a heavy blow to knock a limpet off its rock.

When the sea covers the shore at **high tide,** the limpets crawl over the rocks and eat seaweed. Before the tide has gone out again, each limpet returns to exactly the same spot it was in before it crawled off to eat.

Hermit crabs do not have shells of their own. They live in old, empty shells, such as the whelk shell you see here. The crab holds its coiled body in the shell with some of its legs. It walks on other legs, carrying its borrowed shell around with it. When danger comes near, the crab disappears into the shell and blocks the entrance with one or both of its pincers.

When a hermit crab grows too big for its shell, it hunts for a larger empty shell. When it finds one, it measures it carefully with its legs. If the shell is the right size, the crab climbs out of the old shell and into the new one.

7

Horseshoe crabs are also called king crabs. They have five pairs of legs under their shells. Horseshoe crabs are not really crabs at all. In fact, they are more like spiders. Horseshoe crabs can grow to about a foot (30 centimeters) across the shell.

Horseshoe crabs live on the bottom of the sea. They plough through the sand or mud in search of things to eat. They like worms and **shellfish,** such as clams and mussels. When they find shellfish, the horseshoe crabs use their powerful legs to crush the hard shells.

Every spring, horseshoe crabs walk up to the seashore to lay their eggs. Thousands crowd onto each mile of shore and dig holes where they lay their eggs. When the eggs hatch out, the young crabs are swept by the waves into the sea and swim away.

9

Lugworms live at the bottom of U-shaped burrows in the sand, with an entrance at each end. One entrance of the burrow is marked by a small pit. At the other entrance, there is a small pile of sand, called a **wormcast.** This looks a bit like coiled-up spaghetti. Lugworms are so common on some beaches that it is difficult to walk without stepping on a wormcast.

When the tide is in, lugworms pump water through their burrows. They eat grains of sand and tiny pieces of seaweed and animals that fall into their burrows. It is the remains, which the lugworm pushes up to the surface, that form the wormcasts.

Laughing gulls are named after the noise they make. Like other kinds of gulls, they live on the seashore, where they search for food. They will eat almost anything they can find. They look for worms and other small animals on the beach. They catch fish that swim near the surface of the sea.

Many pairs of gulls nest in groups near the seashore. Large groups of animals living together are called **colonies.** Each pair of gulls builds a nest of grass and seaweed and lays three or four eggs. After the eggs have hatched, the parents bring food to the baby gulls. The parents continue to look after the young gulls, even after the young have learned to fly.

Starfish usually live in deep water. Sometimes they come into **tide pools,** and dead starfish are often found on the beach. They get their name from their star shape. Most have five arms. They have small bodies and no heads. They crawl along the bottom of the sea on dozens of tube feet. These look like tiny, rubbery stilts. The tube feet have suckers that help the starfish climb rocks.

Starfish eat fish, crabs, and **shellfish** such as clams and mussels. The bodies of shellfish are inside the shells. Starfish fasten the suckers of their feet onto the shells and pull them open. Then the starfish push their stomachs through their mouths to digest the bodies of their **prey.**

If a starfish loses any of its arms, it can grow new ones. In fact, a single arm and the body will even grow into a whole new starfish.

Weever fish (above) live in shallow water. They bury themselves in the sand or mud. Their eyes are on the tops of their heads. Even when they are almost buried, they can see. They sometimes catch shrimps that swim past. Weever fish can give a painful sting to anyone who goes wading and steps on one.

Blennies (right) are small, lively fish that feed on small sea animals. Some live in **tide pools.** They hide and sometimes lay their eggs in holes and cracks in rocks or in empty shells. One parent, either the father or the mother, stays with the eggs until they hatch. The parent may attack other fish that come too close.

H arbor (or common) seals spend almost all their lives in the sea. They like to lie in the warm sun, too. They pull themselves out of the sea, up onto the rocks or the beach, using their front flippers. They may sleep there until the tide comes in and then swim away.

Harbor seals have their babies in summer. The female seals find a quiet spot to give birth to their babies. Baby harbor seals, or pups, are able to swim right after they are born, but not strongly. In a few weeks, they are strong enough to dive alongside their mothers.

Prawns and shrimps (above) are common on all sea-shores. They can be found in **tide pools** and in shallow water. Their bodies are **transparent,** like glass, and are very hard to see. They normally swim by paddling with a row of legs called swimmerets. They can move backward quickly by flicking their tails.

Although goose barnacles (right) look a bit like clams or mussels, they are actually more like crabs or prawns. Their many pairs of legs wave, bringing water and food into their shells. In case of danger, the legs can be pulled inside and the shell closed.

One end of a goose barnacle's body is a rubbery stalk. It glues the barnacle to something solid, such as a rock.

G reen turtles live in warm seas. They feed on sea grass and other sea plants. Every year, adult female turtles return to the beaches where they hatched. Some swim 1,200 to 1,800 miles (2,000 to 3,000 km) to get there and lay their eggs. The turtles come ashore at night. They heave their heavy bodies up the beach until they are above the **high-tide** mark. Then they dig holes in the sand with their back flippers. Each female lays about 100 round, white eggs, covers the hole with sand, and returns to the sea.

Eight weeks later, all the eggs hatch at the same time. The baby turtles dig out of the sand and race down the beach to the sea. Before they reach the water, many are eaten by crabs, birds, and other **predators.** The little turtles are safe only when they have swum away from the shore.

The Galapagos Islands in the Pacific Ocean are the home of marine iguanas. These are lizards that grow to over 3 feet (1 meter) long. When the tide goes out, the marine iguanas go along the shore and eat seaweed. The sea around the Galapagos Islands is cool. But the iguanas sunbathe, and their bodies are warm before they go swimming. Iguanas have sharp claws, so they can cling tightly to the rocks and not be thrown around by the waves. Sometimes they swim into deeper water and dive for food. They can stay underwater for twenty minutes or more.

Iguanas lay their eggs on sandy beaches. The females dig 3-foot-long burrows in the sand. They each lay two or three eggs at the far end of their burrows. Then they fill the burrows with sand, and, four months later, the eggs hatch.

23

Index/Glossary

Photo Credits
The publishers wish to thank the following for permission to reproduce copyright material:
Oxford Scientific Films and individual copyright holders on the following pages: G. I. Bernard 4, 5, 6, 7, 10 inset, 18, back cover, Waina Cheng front cover, J. A. L. Cooke 20, Fredrik Ehrenstrom 3, 13, 14, Rodger Jackman 12, Warwick Johnson 22, Animals Animals/Breck P. Kent 2, 9, Rudie Kuiter 15, London Scientific Films 10, Godfrey Merlen title page, 21, Okapia 16–17, W. Pfunder 23, Edward Robinson 8, 11, D.J. Saunders 17, David Shale 19